TIME
FOR KIDS

Anne Frank

A LIGHT IN THE DARK

Tamara Leigh Hollingsworth

Consultants

Timothy Rasinski, Ph.D.
Kent State University

Lori Oczkus
Literacy Consultant

Maureen McNeil
Director of Education,
The Anne Frank Center

Based on writing from
TIME For Kids. *TIME For Kids* and the *TIME For Kids* logo are registered trademarks of TIME Inc. Used under license.

Publishing Credits

Dona Herweck Rice, *Editor-in-Chief*
Lee Aucoin, *Creative Director*
Jamey Acosta, *Senior Editor*
Lexa Hoang, *Designer*
Stephanie Reid, *Photo Editor*
Rane Anderson, *Contributing Author*
Rachelle Cracchiolo, *M.S.Ed., Publisher*

Teacher Created Materials

5301 Oceanus Drive
Huntington Beach, CA 92649-1030
http://www.tcmpub.com

ISBN 978-1-4333-4865-5

© 2013 Teacher Created Materials, Inc.
Printed in China
Nordica.072018.CA21800727

Table of Contents

Chapter 1

An Extraordinary Girl

Every child dreams about the future and wonders what life will be like as an adult. When Anne Frank was a young woman, she thought about what her life would be like when she grew up. Her world was filled with fear. But Anne kept the light of hope in her heart.

Anne was an **outgoing** girl who loved to have fun. She enjoyed when her father's friends came to visit. She made them laugh. Her mother called her "the little comedian." She often got in trouble for speaking her mind at school.

This lively girl was born in Frankfurt, Germany, on June 12, 1929. Her family had lived there for over 100 years. Her father, Otto Frank, ran a successful business. Her mother stayed home with Anne and her older sister, Margot. Like many German families, the Franks were **Jewish**.

But, by 1945, six million Jews were dead. Anne did not survive, but her powerful words did.

THINK LINK

- Who was Anne Frank?
- Why is her writing so important to us today?
- How can we honor her memory?

Imagine hiding silently in an attic for over two years.

Extraordinary Times

The Frank family had lived in Frankfurt for over 300 years. They were successful bankers and business people. They watched as **anti-Semitism** and hostility toward Jews grew. Germany had a **diverse** population. Each group believed something different. But there was a group of people who particularly disliked Jews.

Anne was born just before the **Great Depression**. The Western world was in a **crisis**. Millions of people had lost their jobs. And they were unable to find new ones. People were scared. They wanted someone to blame.

In Germany, a man named Adolf Hitler began giving hate-filled speeches. He blamed Germany's problems on anyone who seemed different. Mostly, he blamed the Jews. In 1933, he led the **Nazi Party**, a powerful political group. Hitler led people to act in hateful ways toward Jews. Many innocent Jewish people were fired from their jobs. Some had to close their businesses. Anne's father decided to leave Frankfurt. He wanted to take his family away from the danger.

During the Great Depression, millions of people lost their jobs in both the United States and Germany.

Hitler's Power

Hitler was a powerful speaker. He told people that if they did what he said without question, they would have money, food, and happiness again. These promises helped Hitler gain power in Germany.

The Frank family moved to Amsterdam, Holland, in 1933. At first, life was calmer. Hitler wasn't powerful there. The Franks believed they were safe. Like all children, Anne attended school. She dreamed of becoming a movie star. But the peace of her childhood did not last.

In May 1940, the Nazis attacked Holland. The Franks had left Frankfurt to escape cruelty toward Jews. But now, they faced the same problems. Hitler created new rules that treated Jews as inferior **outcasts**.

Outsiders

Hitler called Jews *outsiders*. If a book had Jewish ideas or was written by a Jewish person, Hitler ordered it to be burned. Jews were not allowed in places such as restaurants, movie theaters, or schools. It was not only Jews that Hitler targeted. He spoke with hatred against anyone who did not believe the same things he did.

A Nazi soldier stands in front of a store with a sign that reads, "Germans! Defend yourselves! Do not buy from Jews!"

The Star of David

The Star of David is a symbol of the Jewish faith. The 12 sides of the star represent the original 12 Jewish families. Hitler imposed laws that required Jews to wear the star. He wanted it to be easy to pick out Jews so they couldn't hide or try to work together.

Jude is the German word for *Jew*.

Jews were forced to wear the Star of David where it could be easily identified.

Frightening Changes

The Frank family wanted what other people wanted. They wanted to live freely and feel safe. They wanted to be with their loved ones. They hoped for an end to Hitler's hatred toward Jews.

Shattered Dreams

Hitler tried to destroy everything the Jews loved. In 1938, he burned down more than 200 Jewish **synagogues** (SIN-uh-gogs). The streets were covered with the broken glass from the shattered windows. There was so much glass in the streets that the event earned the name *Crystal Night*.

Margot Frank

The Call

When Jews were ordered to report to the Nazis, they received a *call-up letter*. The name was meant to make it sound like a good thing. But people knew it meant they could be going to a work camp. Jewish families were deeply afraid of receiving a call-up letter.

In 1942, Anne turned 13. For her birthday, her father gave her a journal. It would be a safe place to keep all her thoughts. Soon after, Anne's sister, Margot, received a letter. In it, she was ordered to report to a work camp. The Franks knew the people who went there worked so hard they felt barely human. Millions of people who reported to the camps were never heard from again.

Miep Gies

The Franks knew they needed to do something. Otto asked his friend Miep Gies (MEEP GEES) for help. They knew their plan was dangerous. If they were caught, they would be killed. But it was agreed. The Frank family would go into hiding.

Diary of a Young Girl

Is your best friend someone at school? Perhaps it's your neighbor or your pet? During the war, Anne's best friend was her diary. The diary was a **confidant** and a source of comfort during a very dark time in her life. In the diary, she wrote about everyday things, like the food they ate. She also wrote about World War II and how it affected her family. Writing was Anne's passion. She hoped her diary would be published one day. She even edited and rewrote large portions of the book.

Anne created **aliases** for many of the people she wrote about. She was looking ahead to publishing her diary and wanted to protect them.

"The nicest part is being able to write down all my thoughts and feelings; otherwise I'd absolutely suffocate."

—Anne Frank

Anne used a separate notebook to write short stories. She also collected favorite sentences from other writers for inspiration.

Anne wrote her first diary entry on the day of her 13th birthday.

Under Lock and Key

Anne's diary had a gold lock and a key to match. Its cover was red and white gingham, like a picnic tablecloth. She addressed most diary entries to *Kitty*. Starting off an entry with *Dear Kitty* made her feel as if she were writing to a real person. By the end of Anne's first year in hiding, the diary's unlined pages were filled from beginning to end.

Into Hiding

The Franks moved into a tiny apartment hidden above a warehouse. Their new home needed to stay a secret. They couldn't draw any attention to themselves. They couldn't say good-bye to friends. They left many of their belongings behind. But Anne made sure to pack her journal. She later wrote, "Memories mean more to me than dresses."

Saying Good-Bye

Anne was saddest to leave behind her cat, Moortje (MOOR-chya). She wanted to bring her along, but it wasn't safe. Gies went back to the Franks' apartment to check that Moortje was safe.

The warehouse building where the Franks hid in the attic.

Gestapo

The Gestapo was a violent and dangerous police unit. Hitler used the police to make people tell secrets. They did horrible things like pulling Jewish children off the street and sending them to camps. Sometimes, they broke into houses and stole everything. Nobody could stop Hitler because people were terrified of the Gestapo.

Gestapo chief
Heinrich Himmler

Even though it was July, each member of the Frank family "put on **heaps** of clothes." The family couldn't be seen carrying suitcases. They walked through the streets, pretending everything was normal. Every move was designed to help them avoid the **Gestapo** (guh-STAH-poh). When they got to their new home, they walked to the secret entrance.

A bookcase was built to hide the secret entrance to the apartment.

Chapter 2

The Hiding Place

Behind a bookcase lay their new home, the **Secret Annex**. Inside was a small apartment. There were bedrooms and a small kitchen with room for reading. At night, they pushed the bookcase aside. Then, the Franks went downstairs to stretch their legs in safety. Gies's job was to bring the family food and other items they needed while in hiding. Gies wasn't Jewish. She could travel around town freely. Only Gies and a few other people knew the Frank family was hiding there.

The Ultimate Risk

Gies, like other people who helped Jewish families, put herself in great danger. There were laws against aiding Jews in any way. Any person who didn't follow Hitler's rules could be killed.

Jan and Miep Gies, standing by the bookcase entrance in 1987

the office in the warehouse

Gies was aided by other brave employees and friends of the Franks. Victor Kugler, Johannes Kleiman, and Bep Voskuijl helped as well.

Blue Heaven

Sometimes Anne became angry or frustrated living in such tight quarters. But she reminded herself how much worse life could be. She thought of the Annex as "a little piece of blue heaven, surrounded by heavy black rain clouds."

A Hidden World

The Secret Annex was small, but it meant the world to the Franks. Slip behind the bookcase and step inside.

Anne posted pictures of movie stars, art, and royalty on the wall.

Gies gave Anne a pair of red shoes. Anne declared them "exceptionally beautiful!" It was the first time she had worn high heels.

Second floor

Anne admired the large chestnut tree outside the house through these windows.

STOP! THINK...

- What belongings would you bring with you if you needed to hide?

- Which room would you want to be yours?

- Why do you think Anne loved sitting near the windows?

Anne loved to write at this small table.

Third floor

A New Home

The Franks weren't the only people living in the Secret Annex. The van Pels family also lived there with their son, Peter. Later, another Jewish man, Dr. Fritz Pfeffer, came to live with them. Together, these eight people lived in a small **cramped** space. Life in the Annex was difficult. Everyone was forced to follow a strict schedule so they wouldn't be discovered. This included nine hours of silence in the middle of the day. People worked in the factory below and they could not risk being heard. Anne wrote in her diary to pass the time.

Trying to Get Along

Living in such a tight space meant people didn't always get along. Anne struggled to be polite, but there were still sometimes arguments.

the bedroom Anne shared, first with Margot, and then Pfeffer

Staying Quiet

The residents of the Secret Annex stayed safe by following a schedule. They avoided making noise whenever workers were downstairs. Here's what a day might have looked like in the Secret Annex.

6:45 A.M.	Wake up early.
8:30 A.M.	Hide and stay silent as warehouse workers arrive downstairs.
9:00 A.M.	Go upstairs for breakfast when the office employees arrive. Gies checks in on everyone and picks up the shopping list
12:30 P.M.	Breathe a sigh of relief when the warehouse workers go home for lunch.
1:00 P.M.	Listen to the news on the radio while preparing lunch.
2:00 P.M.	Stay as quiet as possible the rest of the day. Take naps, read, and write.
5:30 P.M.	Enjoy the freedom of the night when the office workers have gone home. Spread out into the office space downstairs until dinner.
6:00 P.M.	Dinner is served whenever the radio broadcasts the news.
9:00 P.M.	Get ready for bed.
10:00 P.M.	Go to bed.

The members of the Secret Annex didn't know how long they would be in hiding. Most thought it would only be for a few weeks. But a whole year passed. The war was growing worse. There was little food. The children's clothes and shoes no longer fit. People were tired, sick, and longed to be outside.

In 1942, Hitler made a cruel plan. The **Final Solution** was designed to find Jews and send them to death camps. The rumors were terrifying for the Frank family. But Anne tried to stay hopeful. She wrote in her journal that she wanted to remember to smile more.

Inside Looking Out

Anne once wrote about how it felt to be trapped in hiding. "Not being able to go outside upsets me more than I can say, and I'm terrified our hiding place will be discovered and that we'll be shot."

Hitler and the Nazi leadership

the Nazi invasion

The World Outside

Sometimes at night, Anne could hear bombs dropping on the city or soldiers marching in the streets. When she became afraid, she slept with her parents in their room.

A Hopeful Heart

Terrible things were happening. But those trapped in the Secret Annex tried to keep up their spirits. Anne and Otto wrote silly poems to each other. They all created reasons to celebrate. Anne often set aside her portion of the sugar to make treats. All the while, she and Peter grew closer. They both knew how it felt to live in hiding. After a time, she even began calling him "darling Peter" in her diary.

Anne Frank

The Gift of Writing

Writing poems was a beloved tradition of Dutch families. The poems were often given as gifts and later collected in scrapbooks.

Rationing

During the war, the government limited the amount of food, electricity, and sweets people could have. People were given a card with the amount of things they could buy. **Rationing** was difficult and dangerous for Gies. She was only supposed to shop for two people, yet she had to buy enough groceries for the eight people living in the Secret Annex, too.

a German ration card

Zusatz=Lebensmittel
für Hochzeiten
3 Personen
Ernährungsamt

47066
29.9.44

Ausgegeben am
Nicht übertragbar! Nur gültig für die Dauer von 14 Tagen
Abtrennen nur durch Empfänger der Abschnitte

Gies's kitchen

The Anne Frank Tree

Today, the Anne Frank House is a museum and a place where people around the world visit to honor those who died in the war. Anne loved to spend many hours admiring the large chestnut tree outside the Secret Annex. It was one of the oldest trees in Amsterdam. Its beauty reminded her of freedom. In 2010, the tree had grown so old it could no longer stand. Saplings from the tree have been planted all over the world.

Today, the Anne Frank Tree still lives on in an interactive online **monument**. You can leave a virtual leaf in the tree and tell the world how Anne has inspired you.

"Nearly every morning I go to the attic to blow the stuffy air out of my lungs. From my favorite spot on the floor I look up at the blue sky and the bare chestnut tree, on whose branches little raindrops shine, appearing like silver, and at the seagulls and other birds as they glide on the wind."

—Anne Frank

Good News

In June 1944, there was excitement in the Secret Annex. Radio reports said the **Allied Forces** were now in Europe, fighting Hitler's army. As news of the battles came, Otto tracked their progress on an old map hung on the wall. Anne wrote in her diary that friends were coming to help.

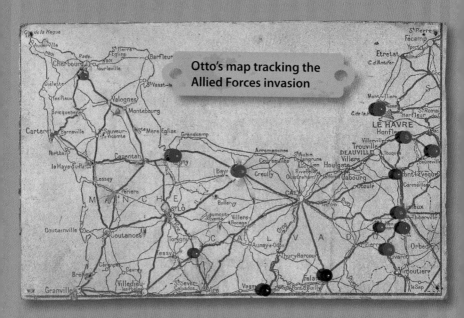

Otto's map tracking the Allied Forces invasion

As the Allies marched through Europe, Hitler and his army became desperate. Afraid he was losing power, Hitler made life more difficult for everyone. The Frank family was in constant danger of being discovered. At one point, thieves broke into the factory and almost found the entrance to the Secret Annex. In fear, everyone stayed silent for two long days.

D-Day

June 6, 1944, is known as D-Day. The Allied Forces stormed the beaches on the northern coast of France. The Allies were moving closer to Germany and Hitler's defeat.

Soldiers threaten Jews.

Extreme Measures

In the final days of the war, Hitler knew he was losing. But he wouldn't go down without a fight. Toward the end, he tried to kill as many Jews as possible before the war ended.

Chapter 3

Arrested

In August 1944, Anne's worst fear came true. Nazi police found the Franks' hiding place. Someone had tipped off the Gestapo. The members of the Secret Annex were each given five minutes to pack one bag. They were arrested and questioned. Then, they were placed on trains and sent to a **concentration camp**. While there, they were able to stay together. But soon, they were put on a train so packed with people there was no room to move. When the train stopped, the men and women were separated. Anne was taken away from her father and Peter. Anne, Margot, their mother, and the other women on the train were forced to walk. They went to a camp for women.

the fence at Auschwitz (OUSH-vits), the deadliest concentration camp in the war

In Hiding

There were about 25,000 Jews hiding in Holland. Through violence and fear, the Gestapo were able to locate around 9,000 of them.

an entry in Anne's diary

Confronting Evil

Anne thought about what was happening in the world around her. She once wrote that "everything is so different from ordinary times and from ordinary people's lives." She wondered what anyone could do in the face of such evil.

The Camps Today

Today, the camps have been turned into museums. Close to one million people travel to Europe to see the camps in person. Many of Hitler's war papers can be seen in the museums.

Life as Prisoners

Life in the concentration camp was **horrific**. The prisoners were treated cruelly. Like everyone there, Anne's hair was shaved off. All her personal belongings were taken from her. She was forced to wear a gray fabric sack that did little to keep out the cold. Soon, Anne and Margot were moved away from their mother to the Bergen-Belsen camp. There, both Anne and Margot caught **typhus** (TAHY-fuhs). In March 1945, at just 15 years old, Anne died.

Only a few weeks after her death, the Nazis **surrendered**. The Allied Forces traveled to each of the concentration camps and freed the prisoners. Otto Frank was the only person from the Secret Annex to survive the **Holocaust**. (HOL-uh-kawst). After the war, he went to live with Gies and her husband in Amsterdam.

prisoners in line

Typhus

Typhus is spread by lice and fleas. It causes painful stomachaches and a high fever. Because it is spread by bugs that are difficult to control, the disease spreads easily.

Two Lines

At the entrance to Hitler's concentration camps, people were separated into two lines. The healthy and strong were sent into one line. They were kept alive for **manual labor**. The other line was for anyone thought to be old or weak. They were put to death immediately.

the Auschwitz train station

Hitler's Victims

Anne was one of the millions of lives lost during the Holocaust. By the time the war was over, Hitler and the Nazis had killed 11 million people. Auschwitz was the worst of all the camps. It was known as a *death camp*.

Margot died of typhus just a few days before Anne did.

The Strength Within

What gave people the strength to go on? No matter how bad things were, the hope of freedom kept them alive. For some, it was the hope that Hitler would be defeated. Many people were **resistance fighters** who rescued Jews and fought the Nazis any way they could. Others had something they wanted to live for. Parents wanted to live for their children. Musicians, artists, and writers wanted to continue their work. Being hopeful helped many of them survive.

Viktor Frankl

Something to Live For

Viktor Frankl was another Holocaust survivor. He noticed the people who had hope were the people who had a reason to survive. After the war, he wrote a famous book titled *Man's Search for Meaning*. It was about how people had a greater chance of surviving if they have something or someone to live for.

Another Survivor

David Bram was first sent to a labor camp and then to concentration camps. He worked hard because he wanted to survive to see his family again. He was liberated from the camp by American troops. After the war, he moved to America. When he tells about his time in the camps, he says he often told himself, "As long as my heart beats, I will never give up."

Jubilant prisoners celebrate their freedom from a concentration camp.

Chapter 4

Anne's Voice

After the Franks were arrested and taken away, Gies found Anne's journal. She protected it for more than two years. When the war was over, she returned it to Anne's father. Otto was proud of her words. He told the world she stood for all those who suffered because of their beliefs, color, or race. Anne lived during a time when hatred, **prejudice**, and cruelty seemed to be everywhere. But she refused to let that become part of who she was. She was like any normal girl. She fought with her family. She decorated her room with posters of movie stars and dreamed of what her life would be. And even though she saw how cruel people could be, she remained hopeful. In her diary, she wrote, "In spite of everything, I still believe people are good at heart."

Dear Diaries

Anne wasn't the only child to write about the war. Other children kept diaries about their life in hiding. So why did Anne's become the most famous? Is it because she was a "little comedian"? Is it because her friendly personality makes us feel as if we know her? Or perhaps it's because her strength is inspirational. Whatever the reason, Anne captured the heart of the world. Through her words, she will live forever.

Mass Grave

Anne and Margot were buried with thousands of others in a **mass grave**. This stone at a camp honors them, but it isn't where they are buried.

Remembering Anne

"I want to go on living even after my death," Anne wrote in her diary. Today, every year, nearly one million people visit the Secret Annex where Anne hid for 25 months. They walk through the bookcase door and step into the past. There, they can see Anne's diary. They see where her family spent their days. They feel how tight the space was and try to imagine what it was like to hide there. Together, the world keeps Anne's memory alive.

Otto holds an award given after Anne's diary sold more than a million copies worldwide.

Anne's diary has been published around the world in multiple languages.

Otto Frank

Telling the World

Otto wanted to share Anne's hope with the world. Anne's diary was first published in 1947 as *The Secret Annex*. In 1952, it was published in the United States. In 1955, a play based on Anne's diary was written. The play was also turned into an award-winning film.

Time Line of Anne Frank's Life

1940
Hitler's Nazi army
attacks Holland.

1941
All Jews in Holland
are forced to wear
the Star of David.

1929
Anne is born in
Frankfurt, Germany.

1942
Anne receives her
journal as a birthday
present from her father.

1942
The Frank family
goes into hiding.

1944
The Secret Annex
is discovered.

1945
Anne dies of typhus in
the Bergen-Belsen camp.

"We're all alive, but we don't know why or what for; we're all searching for happiness; we're all leading lives that are different and yet the same."

–Anne Frank

1947
Anne's diary is published under the title *The Secret Annex*.

1945
The Nazis surrender.

1957
Otto Frank helps establish the Anne Frank Foundation.

1960
The Anne Frank House opens in Amsterdam.

Glossary

aliases—invented names used to hide the identity of a writer or the identity of those whom the writer is writing about

Allied Forces—Great Britain, France, Russia, and later the United States; the group of countries that fought against Germany in World War II

anti-Semitism—hostility or prejudice in feelings, speech, or actions toward Jews

concentration camp—a place during World War II where Jews and other "outsiders" were collected and forced to work or be killed

confidant—someone you can tell secrets to

cramped—tight

crisis—a time when things are extremely unstable and unsafe

diverse—to be made up of all different types

Final Solution—the Nazi program designed to kill all Jews

Gestapo—the secret police of Nazi Germany

Great Depression—the economic crisis and period of low business activity in the United States and other countries, beginning with the stock market crash in 1929, and continuing through most of the 1930s

heaps—large amounts

Holocaust—the mass killing of European Jews in Nazi concentration camps during World War II

horrific—causing horror, or an overwhelming pain and fear caused by something terrible

Jewish—relating to the religion of Judaism

manual labor—physically intense work

mass grave—a grave containing many unidentified bodies

monument—something created in memory of someone or an event

Nazi Party—the political party led by Hitler

outcasts—people who are not accepted by society

outgoing—to be talkative and open with people; not shy

prejudice—to judge another person based on how they are different, often because of racial or religious differences

rationing—rules that limit how much of something a person can have

resistance fighters—people who fought against the Nazis

Secret Annex—a small hidden addition to a building

surrendered—gave up

synagogues—Jewish places of worship

typhus—a serious disease spread by lice and fleas

Index

Bibliography

Auerbacher, Inge. *I Am a Star: Child of the Holocaust.* **Puffin, 1993.**

This is an autobiography of a girl who was in a concentration camp with her family for three years, beginning when she was seven. It tells of being forced to wear a yellow star and continues through her years at the camp until the family was freed.

Frank, Anne. *The Diary of a Young Girl: Definitive Edition.* **Bantam, 1997.**

Read about Anne's life in her own words. This is the translated version of the published diary that Anne Frank wrote in Dutch.

Lee, Carol Ann. *Anne Frank's Story: Her Life Retold for Children.* **Troll Communications, 2002.**

This book tells of Anne Frank's life before, during, and after her time in hiding. It includes photographs of the Frank family and the Secret Annex.

Lowry, Lois. *Number the Stars.* **Houghton Mifflin Harcourt, 1989.**

This novel, based on facts, tells the story of a Danish family that protected Jews and helped them escape the Nazis. It is told through the eyes of a 10-year-old girl whose family is helping her best friend's family leave the country.

Zullo, Allan and Mara Bovsun. *Survivors: True Stories of Children in the Holocaust.* **Scholastic Paperbacks, 2005.**

This book contains the accounts of nine Jewish boys and girls who lived through the Holocaust.

More to Explore

Anne Frank Center
http://www.annefrank.com

Located in New York City, this non-profit organization educates students about tolerance, the Holocaust, and Anne Frank's legacy.

Anne Frank House
http://www.annefrank.org

This website includes an interactive time line and an online tour of the house in which they were hidden.

The Children of the Holocaust
http://thechildrenoftheholocaust.com/

This website includes topics such as tolerance for kids, Holocaust survivors, diversity activities, and Holocaust facts.

The Museum of Tolerance
http://www.museumoftolerance.com

Explore biographies of children from World War II as well as a time line of the Holocaust.

Students Against Violence Everywhere
http://www.nationalsave.org/

SAVE is a student-driven organization. At the SAVE website, you will learn about alternatives to violence, conflict management skills, and the virtues of good citizenship, civility, and nonviolence. You can practice what you learn through school and community-service projects.

About the Author

Tamara Leigh Hollingsworth was born and raised in Cupertino, California. She attended Hollins University, where she earned a degree in English. She has been a high school English teacher for many years. She currently lives in Atlanta, Georgia. When she is not working with her beloved students, Tamara loves to spend time with her husband, her daughter, and her books—especially biographies.

Visitors at the Anne Frank House examine a replica of the Annex.